HOW ARE THEY BUILT?

ROADS & HIGHWAYS

Lynn M. Stone

Rourke Publishing LLC
Vero Beach, Florida 32964

www.rourkepublishing.com

PHOTO CREDITS:
© Corel: cover; © Corbis: page 8; © Al Michaud: page 11; © Armentrout: pages 16, 34; © Finlay McNary Engineers, Inc.:page 24; © Bill Sciallo:pages 26, 36; © Dynamic Designs: pages 18, 28, 30, 31, 42; © PhotoDisc, Inc.: pages 4, 6, 12, 20, 22; ©Cory Heintz, Iowa Department of Transportation: pages 38, 39, 41

EDITORIAL SERVICES:
Pamela Schroeder

ABOUT THE AUTHOR:
Lynn Stone is the author of more than 400 children's books. He is a talented natural history photographer as well. Lynn, a former teacher, travels worldwide to photograph wildlife in its natural habitat.

Library of Congress Cataloging-in-Publication Data

Stone, Lynn M.
    Roads and highways / Lynn M. Stone
       p cm. — (How are they built?)
    Includes bibliographical references and index.
    Summary: Discusses how roads are built in the United States, presenting some historical background and giving specific examples.
      ISBN 1-58952-138-2
       1. Roads—Designs and construction—Juvenile literature. [1. Roads—Design and construction.] I. Title

TE149 .S76 2001
624.7'097—dc21   2001041651

Printed In The USA

TABLE OF CONTENTS

Millions of miles of roads in North America make travel easier and faster.

ROADS

North Americans really love—and hate—their roads. Sometimes roads are crowded with traffic jams. Some roads are ugly, or built in places where they are not needed. Even well-built roads can be dangerous.

But roads take us where we want to go, from countryside to city, from city to city, and beyond. For better or worse, roads, and the cars and trucks that drive over them, have shaped the North American lifestyle. Roads have become fast tracks to the places where we find history, nature, adventure, and business. Roads provide North Americans fast, easy, and cheap **access** to goods, services, and each other.

Roads like this one in the Florida Keys stand as monuments to modern engineering.

Roads give us pathways to some of the most amazing sights in North America. Roads can take us within a snowball's throw of mighty glaciers. Roads span wild rivers, skirt waterfalls, and snake along seashore cliffs. On Florida's Overseas Highway you can take a road over the sea. Further north, you can take a road that travels over and under Chesapeake Bay, an arm of the Atlantic Ocean.

Everyone knows what a road is, but roads have many names: lane, drive, avenue, street, boulevard, highway, freeway, parkway, tollway, thoroughfare, pike, and **turnpike**, for example. In some cases, a name means a special kind of road. A tollway, for example, is a modern highway on which toll money is collected. A tollway is not likely to be confused with an avenue, although it might be confused with a freeway. Freeways are modern, high-speed highways, but they are not always free. And *tollway* could also be confused with *turnpike*, which may also be a toll road. America's most famous turnpike, the Pennsylvania, is a toll road. But the old Berlin Turnpike, in Connecticut, is not.

The name chosen for a road often has something to do with where it is. While *turnpike* and *parkway* have their roots in the East, *freeway* is more of a California term. When Californians travel east, the Pennsylvania Turnpike is just another freeway with tolls.

You would never call the modern, multi-lane highways of the American Interstate System avenues or drives. We tend to think of avenues and drives as quiet, tree-lined streets. They often are, but the name, again, can be misleading. Have you ever seen loud, bustling Fifth Avenue in downtown New York City? Have you seen rush-hour traffic on the many lanes of Lake Shore Drive in Chicago?

Whatever you call it, a road is just what it is—a pathway made for vehicles.

Chicago's Lake Shore Drive was built with many lanes to handle heavy traffic.

HISTORY OF ROADS

Roads have been around much longer than the cars and trucks that rush over them today. While roads today are designed for motorized vehicles, they were once designed for horses, wagons, carriages, and marching armies. The 20th century produced a huge explosion of road building to handle all the motorized vehicles. But roads first appeared not long after the wheel, some 5,000 years ago. The Old Silk Trade Road traveled 6,000 miles (9,600 km) to connect China with Rome and other parts of Europe.

Always skilled **engineers**, the ancient Romans were the first really good road builders. They knew how to make **pavements** of flat stones. They built roads with a center **crown** for rain control and dug roadside ditches to carry water away. Hundreds of years before cars, the Romans built more than 50,000 miles (80,000 km) of roads in their empire. Some of them are still being used!

France began building gravel and stone roads in the early 1700s. A hundred years later, Scotch engineer John L. McAdam invented the **macadam** surface for roads. McAdam's pavement was so good, it's still being used.

Meanwhile, in the United States, the first road wide enough for stage coaches to travel between New York City and Boston was finished in 1722. The first hard-surfaced road in America was built in 1794. It was the Lancaster Turnpike, a 62-mile (100-km) toll road from Lancaster, Pennsylvania, to Philadelphia. Tolls ranged from 1 cent to 13 1/2 cents per mile. The rate depended upon the size of the wagon and how many horses were pulling it.

Some roads built by ancient Romans are still in use today.

*Before modern pavement was invented, bricks were
often used in road construction.*

After Pennsylvania's Lancaster Turnpike, several more were built in the next 40 years. They were built with surfaces of gravel or broken stones. Some American roads, however, were being paved with planks, logs, wood blocks, bricks, or **cobblestones**.

By the mid-1850s, you could travel by road from New York to San Francisco. Some did. But it was, at best, a 3-week wagon ride just to go from St. Louis to San Francisco. By the close of the 19th century, the United States had more than 2 million miles of roads. Most of them were dirt roads, dusty and very bumpy.

When cars and bicycles became popular early in the 20th century, road building became more important. Old U.S. Route 30 was built as the Lincoln Highway between 1914 and 1927. It had a concrete surface, and it traveled from the east coast to the west. In 1940 the first part of the Pennsylvania Turnpike opened. It was the first true superhighway in the United States.

The Interstate Highway Act was passed in Congress in 1944, as World War II was coming to an end. It set the stage for the great interstate system of highways in the United States. But it was under President Dwight D. Eisenhower, in 1956, that the federal government began to aggressively build the 43,000-mile (68,800-km) Interstate Highway System. Eisenhower had seen Germany's Autobahn highway system during the war, and he was impressed. By 1990 the Interstate Highway System was almost finished.

The United States has a great interstate system of highways.

WHO BUILDS ROADS?

Except for a handful of private roads, roads in North America are built by governments. Local roads are built by the governments of cities, counties, and townships. Highways are built by the states and the federal government. The federal government, in fact, first began providing money to the states for highways in 1916. Washington knew interstate roads would be good for mail, commerce, national defense, and the **welfare** of American society. We build roads for the same reasons today.

*Governments raise money for roads through tolls,
gasoline taxes, and income taxes.*

The federal government continues to fund highways in the United States, often in a big way. About 90 percent of the Interstate Highway System was paid for with federal money. The U.S. government also chips in billions each year for smaller highways.

All of the government dollars used in road work are from taxes. Taxes on each gallon of gasoline, for example, are used for highway funds. Some states, like Illinois, Indiana, Ohio, New York, and New Jersey, have major toll roads. Tolls are another way for governments to raise money for road projects. Property taxes, income taxes, and the sale of **bonds** also add to road funds.

When governments decide they need a road, they begin planning its construction. Road planning is the job of engineers. Highway engineers have to decide on a route that has more advantages than disadvantages. Will the road reduce the costs of the traffic? Will it hurt the environment? Will its benefits, such as greater safety and ease, outweigh the costs of construction, repair, and environmental impact? When an engineer looks at a road route with a hill in the way, for example, the engineer must make a decision. Is the shorter, straighter route—through a tunnel—going to be worth its greater expense?

It can take years to plan, design, and build a highway.

Engineers have more questions, too. What is the ground like on which this new road will be built? Will extra soil have to be hauled to the site? How much private property will have to be bought for the road? How will the **topography** of the route affect the road's design and cost? Are there buildings to go around? How many **culverts**, bridges, and tunnels will be needed?

Engineers work with highway planners who get information from the government and the public. Public hearings are held to see if local people agree with where the new road will be built.

Engineers consult with **geologists** to see what kind of ground they will be building upon. They study photos of the route to see the road as part of the environment as a whole. Finally, the engineers draw up plans from which **contractors**, the road builders, can work.

*American roads climb rugged mountains, cross vast prairies,
and follow scenic coastlines.*

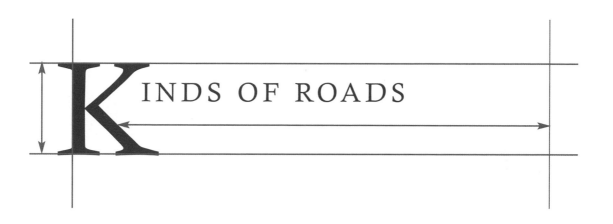

KINDS OF ROADS

There are about 4 million miles (6.2 million km) of roads in the United States and another 550,000 miles (880,000 km) in Canada. Together, American and Canadian roads could wrap around the Earth about 175 times.

Paved roads, which make up the majority of roads in North America, have a fixed, finished surface. Unpaved roads are "dirt" roads or roads with no more than loose gravel or crushed stone as their surface. Some North American roads are broad and made of smooth concrete or blacktop. Others are rocky, rutted, Jeep trails.

Highway route numbers help drivers find their way.

Roads are grouped by their use as well as the kind of pavement. State maps show the types of roads with different colors and line sizes. You should always consult a map's key to find out the status of a road.

Local roads begin and end within a community. They carry local, or city, traffic. Small highways link towns and local roads to bigger highways. Highways are the backbone of North American business. The best examples of highways in North America are the Interstate System of the United States and the Trans Canada Highway.

In the United States, many roads have route numbers assigned to them. The first routes were numbered in the 1920s. East-west routes have an even number. North-south routes have an odd number. U.S. Route 30, for example, is an east-west highway. Interstate 75 (I-75) travels north-south from Michigan to Miami.

The Interstate Highway System is the best of American road building. The interstate highways are designed to be fast and safe. They connect the majority of American cities with populations greater than 50,000. This highway system carries about 21 percent of all traffic in the United States.

Engineers use bridges to allow traffic to flow on and off elevated highways.

What makes a highway part of the Interstate Highway System? As a minimum, a highway in the system must have at least two lanes in both directions. In urban areas, such as Boston and Chicago, the roadways have six or eight lanes. A strip called a **median** divides the two sets of **parallel** lanes. The one-way flow of traffic on each side of the median, the lack of traffic lights, and limited access make the interstates much safer than other highways.

Non-interstate highways, especially older ones, do not have limited access. There are many places where a driver can exit or enter the highway. There are also many **junctions**, or intersections, places where other roads cross the highway. Interstates cross over or under other roads. That increases safety by avoiding traffic lights or stop signs. A driver on the interstate system can travel from New York to Los Angeles without seeing a traffic light.

Roads that enter or exit an interstate highway are well-marked well before the actual turn. They are designed to handle high-speed exits and entrances of traffic. Many of the access points on interstates are designed like giant cloverleaves. Bridges help make the cloverleaf access points. Interstate entry access roads sweep upward to the level of the interstate. Exit traffic curves downward to the intersecting road.

*Road construction crews use special equipment to
make their job easier.*

26

ROADS vs. NATURE

When planning, engineers must keep in mind the forces that will affect the highway. Pavement, for example, must be strong enough to support the weight it carries. Highways that will support trucks need to be stronger than other highways. Pavement helps shift the weight of traffic so that the **roadbed** below the pavement—as well as the pavement itself—can support it. Pavement strength depends upon the building materials, the pavement's thickness, and the roadbed under it. Sand and gravel make stronger roadbeds than clay or silt.

*Ditches and culverts built next to roads keep water
from pooling on the road surface.*

Sooner or later, highways begin to break down and need repair. Pavement begins to crack and crumble, leaving holes and rough spots. The biggest problem for highways is commercial trucking. That is one reason why heavy trucks pay high highway use taxes.

One natural force that concerns highway engineers is water. Wherever a road is built, there is already a natural way that water drains. It may be along a hillside, or through a brook, pond, or the soil. The water in an area and how it moves in its environment is called **hydrology**. Engineers need to know about the hydrology where they plan to build a road. Engineers do not want water to **erode** the highway, so they try to let the water drain the way it did before the road was built. Water needs a place to go. Without a place to drain, it may flood a road or seep underneath pavement. Where there are rivers or streams, engineers can control water by building bridges. Bridges are high enough to allow normal, seasonal flooding to pass underneath them, not over them. Roadside ditches and culverts help keep water away from roads, too.

*Bridges are usually built high enough so that
flooding will not be a problem.*

*Cold or heat can cause road pavement to crack
and pot holes to form.*

31

Cold or heat can cause road surfaces to move and crack. Builders of concrete highways solve this problem by building joints between sections of concrete. That allows the sections to shift without breaking against each other.

In the North, road pavement sometimes breaks because of frost beneath the pavement. As water freezes, it expands, creating more pressure on the pavement than it can stand. Repairing frost damage, however, is cheaper than trying to build a highway that would be frost-proof.

BUILDING ROADS

Road construction begins after the engineers' plans are finished. The construction crew's first job is to clear a right of way—the road's path. Earth-moving machines, like bulldozers, carve a rough roadway by bowling down trees, stumps, rocks, and rough spots in the earth.

Scrapers level the land leaving a rough roadbed.

After bulldozers clear the roadway, the process of rough grading begins. Earth-moving machines—scrapers, among them—move soil up and down, forming a rough roadbed. Machines also pack the new roadbed and tidy up its shape and level. On a modern six-lane, divided highway in rolling country, trucks and machines may dig and transport about 350,000 tons (318,500 metric tons) of soil per mile!

Above the roadbed, construction crews add material to form the road's base. The base supports the road surface. It can be sand, stone, **Portland cement**, or **bitumen**. A 4 to 12-inch (10 to 30-cm) layer of gravel is added as part of the base. Heavy machines known as rollers rumble their huge rolling wheels over the gravel to pack it down.

Paving forms a surface, or pavement, over the roadbed and base. Paving begins with a layer of crushed stone being laid over the gravel. Rollers press the rock into the gravel.

Road construction crews must know how to operate many kinds of heavy equipment.

The gravel and stone base of a road has to be bound, which is a bit like adding glue to all the loose bits of rock. A road's location, its traffic load, and its budget all help engineers decide how to pave it. Paving material can include some chemicals, lime, cement, bitumen, and concrete. On low-traffic roads, pavements are made with gravel, crushed stone, or oyster shell (marl). This base is then covered with a thin layer of hot bitumen called **sealcoat**. You might call it tar or asphalt.

Another surface is made of bituminous macadam. It's a thicker layer of bitumen placed on a bed of crushed stone or gravel. Mixing bitumen with sand, gravel, or crushed stone creates an even better quality surface. This kind of surface is laid by a paving machine, then rolled hard and smooth. It's known as blacktop.

Gravel is used to prepare the base of a roadbed.

Paving machines are used to lay blacktop or concrete onto a road's surface.

Some major highways have a blacktop surface. Most have concrete. Concrete is a mixture of cement, sand, water, and gravel or crushed stone. In its freshly-mixed, liquid form, concrete pours like thick syrup. When it dries, it has incredible strength and rigidity. In highway construction, concrete is poured into forms placed above the road's base. A concrete mixer lays the concrete in long sections. A spreader levels the concrete. Then wires are set into the wet concrete. Another layer of concrete is poured over the wire, which strengthens the concrete. A finishing machine smoothes the concrete and shapes it.

Forms hold wet cement in place.

Guard rails are one of the final details to be added to a road.

Pockets of air and water in the concrete are flushed out with a mechanical float. While it is still wet, the surface of the pavement is dragged with brooms or burlap to form a rough, **textured** surface. A too-smooth finish would be slippery—and dangerous.

Among the final details for construction crews are line-making and adding traffic signals, signs, guard rails, and route markers.

Federal Interstate System, U.S.A. Led by President Eisenhower, the Interstate System covers some 43,000 miles (68,800 km) of America with a network of fast, safe superhighways.

Overseas Highway, Florida Keys. Like a roadway on stilts, the scenic Overseas Highway travels from the tip of the Florida mainland to Key West, 113 miles (181 km) away. Much of the roadway is built on bridges across the blue-green seas where the Gulf of Mexico and Atlantic Ocean meet.

U.S. Route 101, Oregon. Route 101 runs from Brookings to Astoria, often within close view of Oregon's rocky Pacific Coast. Another scenic part of 101 stretches from Orick, California, north through Redwood National Park to Oregon.

Going-to-the-Sun Road, Glacier National Park, Montana. This 50-mile (80-km) road through Glacier National Park goes through some of the most beautiful mountain country in America. But it's not for the faint of heart. Near Logan Pass, the road barely clings to rocky mountainsides.

Trail Ridge Road, Rocky Mountain National Park, Colorado. Trail Ridge is probably the highest paved road in North America. It climbs as high as 12,183 feet (3,713 m), well above tree line, in the snow-capped Colorado Rockies.

Blue Ridge Parkway, Virginia and North Carolina. The beautiful Blue Ridge is a 469-mile (750-km) parkway through the Blue Ridge Range of the Southern Appalachians. It dips to 646 feet (197 m) and rises to 6,410 feet (1,954 m) as it connects the Shenandoah and Great Smoky Mountains National Parks. There are no billboards to detract from the mountainous beauty of the area.

Icefields Parkway, Alberta, Canada. The spectacular 143-mile (229-km) Icefields Parkway links Lake Louise in Banff National Park with the town of Jasper in Jasper National Park. It curls within walking distance of glaciers, lakes, waterfalls, snow-capped peaks, mountain trails, and numerous campgrounds.

Alaska (Alcan) Highway, Alaska, Yukon Territory, British Columbia. The original Alaska Highway, nearly 1,700 miles (2,720 km) long, was built by Canada and the United States in 8 months during 1942. Japan had invaded Alaska's Aleutian Islands and the highway was built as a military supply route from the lower 48 states to Alaska. Today the road is paved—not quite the driving adventure it once was. It is still the only highway from Alaska to Canada and the Lower 48.

Pan American Highway, United States, Mexico, South America. The famous Pan American Highway is really a 29,525-mile (47,516-km) network of highways that allows drivers to go from the United States deep into South America. The road passes through 17 national capitals in Latin America. In the U.S., you can reach the Pan American in Nogales, Arizona, or from one of three Texas cities—Eagle Pass, Laredo, or El Paso.

Trans Canada Highway, Canada. The Trans Canada links 10 Canadian provinces as it reaches from St. John's, Newfoundland, in the east to Victoria, British Columbia, in the west. The toll-free highway can be crowded in cities, but is smooth, quick, and scenic on much of its journey.

Route 1, California. From Obispo to Carmel and again from San Francisco north to Fort Bragg, Route 1 provides one of America's favorite and most famous scenic seaside drives.

GLOSSARY

access (AK ses) — the ability to get into or join; to be able to get to one system from another

bitumen (bih TOO men) — any of several tar-like substances, such as asphalt

bond (BOND) — a certificate sold by the government to make money

cobblestone (KAH bul stohn) — a naturally rounded stone, once popular in road building

contractor (KAHN trak ter) — a person or company that is hired to construct a road or part of it

crown (KROWN) — the high, center point on road pavement that may be slightly curved to allow water to drain

culvert (KUL vert) — an open pipe placed under roads to allow the flow of water

engineer (en jeh NEER) — one who applies science and math to the design of various structures

erode (ih ROHD) — to wear away

geologist (jee AHL eh jist) — a scientist who studies the Earth

hydrology (hy DRAHL eh jee) — the water systems in any area and how they function; the science of studying the actions of water in the environment

junction (JUNGK shen) — the place at which two things come together, such as roads

macadam (meh KAD em) — a type of hard road surface using small stones with a binder, usually asphalt; a road surface named for its inventor, John McAdam

median (MEE dee en) — a strip of land that divides parallel roads

parallel (PAYR EH lel) — that which follows alongside a path or course always at the same distance apart, like rails of a train track

pavement (PAYV ment) — the surface of a road, especially a constructed surface

Portland cement (POHRT land si MENT) — a type of cement that resembles in its makeup the limestone of the Isle of Portland, England

roadbed (ROHD bed) — the hard surface on which a road is built

sealcoat (SEEL koht) — a coating of asphalt used to seal cracks

textured (TEKS cherd) — to have a structured finish as opposed to a perfectly smooth finish

topography (te PAHG reh fee) — the formation of a land surface; the lay of the land with all its hills, valleys, rivers, etc.

turnpike (TURN pyk) — traditionally a toll road, named for the old toll barriers of that name

welfare (WEL fayr) — the well-being or health of someone or something

INDEX

Further Reading:
Armentrout, David and Patricia. *Road Builders*. Rourke, 1995
Brown, Tricia. *The World Famous Alaska Highway*. Fulcrum, 2000
McMurty, Larry. *Driving America's Great Highways*.
Simon & Schuster, 2000

Websites to Visit:
www.aaroads.com/kick-off/highway
www.cahighways.org
www.tfhrc.gov/pubrds/summer96/p96su10

DATE DUE

DEC 0 3 2008		
SEP 1 7 2010		

FOLLETT